Way Maker

AN ADVENT STUDY THROUGH
THE BOOK OF HEBREWS

By
Erin H. Warren

contents

start here

If I had designed the ancient temple in Jerusalem, I probably would have created beautiful marble steps leading up it. You know, like the ones leading up to the great libraries or monuments. But that's not how the steps leading to the temple in Jerusalem were built.

The steps leading up to the temple are all different lengths, heights, and depths. It may look like an accident, but it was designed this way on purpose. The mismatched steps force temple visitors to look down, watch their step, and enter with reverence. One couldn't just run up the steps and rush into the temple. They had to do so with intention.

That is how I view Advent: a season to slow down and take in the wonder and miracle of Jesus' birth; a season of reflection and anticipation. The word *advent* comes from the Latin word *adventus* which means "coming". Traditionally, it started as believers looked toward the Second Coming of Christ, but over time it has come to include not only His birth at Christmas, but our coming to Him for salvation as well. While my Advent typically doesn't look like a traditional Advent (one year I bought candles, determined to light them, but never bought candle holders, so …), I do make a habit of approaching the season as worshippers would approach the temple: slowly, intentionally, and reverently.

I feel like we often love to focus on the sweet Baby Jesus, lying there in a manger, wrapped in pure white cloths, with stars all around, and animals quietly lying down next to Him. But over the years, I've come to view Christmas through the eye of Easter. Easter was His purpose for coming to begin with, so Christmas and Easter will forever be intertwined. Philippians 2:5-8 says:

> *Have this mind among yourselves, which is yours in Christ Jesus, who, though he was in the form of God, did not count equality with God a thing to be grasped, but emptied himself, by taking the form of a servant, being born in the likeness of men. And being found in human form, he humbled himself by becoming obedient to the point of death, even death on a cross.*

He humbly took all of His God power and constrained it into the form of a baby. He came down. To us. Not as a great king, but as a servant. And He died on the cross. For us.

At first glance, that sounds like an awesome deal for us; I'm really thankful for the big favor. The truth is, Jesus came for so much more. He came to make a way. Yes, a way to forgiveness; a way to hope; a way to joy. But it's more than Him making a way through our problems, challenges, and difficult circumstances. Jesus' coming wasn't to part the Red Sea before us but rather part the divide between us and God, between us and Heaven. Jesus is our Way Maker.

He did not come to make life easy. No, His coming was the greatest act of humility. Because He loves us so much.

I want to spend this Advent season remembering Him this way. And there's no greater book to show us how Jesus made a way than the book of Hebrews.

WHY HEBREWS?

In Exodus, as the Israelites were wandering in the wilderness, God gave them a way for Him to dwell in their midst. God is holy, and we are not. In order for us to have communion with a holy, pure, righteous God, we must be made clean. God provided this way through a sacrificial system in the Tabernacle. Through a series of sacrifices, cleansing, and prayers, the priests would go before God on behalf of the people. They interceded for the people. This continued for hundreds of years, eventually moving to the permanent temple in Jerusalem; but then came Jesus. He did what the blood of bulls and goats could not do: He finished the work once and for all.

Hebrews is a book written to show how Jesus is the fulfillment of the law. The author uses the word *shadow*—that these things are not the true form but instead point us to truth. In fact, if you trace the steps through the Tabernacle, they form the shape of a cross. Hebrews is often called the fifth gospel, and no other book gives us a more concise picture of what Jesus did in making a way for us.

CONTEXT

Anytime we prepare to study a book of the Bible, it's important to set the lens through which we study. The Bible is a book written for us, but we were not the original audience. It helps us better interpret Scripture when we understand first and foremost what it meant to the original audience.

We do not know who wrote the book of Hebrews, but we know it was written around 68 AD, before the destruction of the temple in 70 AD. The Greeks during this time in history would start their letters or persuasive speeches by establishing their own credibility. This is why Paul's letters often start with "Paul, a servant of Christ." Paul was stating why the recipients of his letter should listen.

In contrast, the author of Hebrews wasn't trying to establish who he was, but rather who Jesus was and why they should look to Jesus:

Long ago, at many times and in many ways, God spoke to our fathers by the prophets, but in these last days he has spoken to us by his Son, whom he appointed the heir of all things, through whom also he created the world. He is the radiance of the glory of God and the exact imprint of his nature, and he upholds the universe by the word of his power. After making purification for sins, he sat down at the right hand of the Majesty on high, having become as much superior to angels as the name he has inherited is more excellent than theirs.

Hebrews 1:1-4

I love that the author doesn't name himself. It's like saying, "It's not about me. It's about Him." He starts with Jesus.

This was a time of intense persecution in the church. Nero was emperor of the Roman Empire and he was known for his persecution of Jews. In 64 AD, it grew to its height as he blamed Christians for the burning of Rome. Tensions between Jewish religious leaders and Christians were high, and I can imagine doubts among this new church may have been rising as well. The author of Hebrews wrote these words to encourage Jewish Christians and remind them of who Jesus is and what He did. He's calling them (and us) to move forward and not turn back.

THE PLAN

I'm embarrassed to tell you how many half-filled-in Advent books I have. It's such a busy season with so many activities, and it usually doesn't take long for me to fall behind. So I wanted this journal, this guide through Hebrews, to be doable for Advent. There are 13 readings each between 4-10 verses. You can do them in 13 days or, as I like to do, linger in each passage for a couple of days. Take two days to meditate on the verses and listen to them in your car while driving. Do not worry about cramming it in before Christmas. Technically, the Christmas season doesn't end until Epiphany on January 6.

My passion is inductive Bible study and equipping women with the tools to discover God's character in Scripture. Because of that, I want to keep this book simple, not focusing on my words, but helping guide you toward the simple truths of who God is in the book of Hebrews. Each day consists of four simple actions:

Write it out.

I love writing Scripture! There's something so powerful in writing out verses as I study. I pay attention to each word and often catch things I would otherwise miss. I encourage you to read the entire chapter, but really focus on the selected verses.

What does this tell us about Jesus?

The Bible is not a book about us; it's a book about Him. His character is written across every page, in every verse. Take a few moments to jot down the characteristics of God you see here. To help you, I have a list of names and characteristics of God on pages 12-13. I know there are some separate roles for each person of the Trinity, but to keep things simple, this list includes God the Father, God the Son, and God the Holy Spirit.

How is He the Way Maker?

Read the selected verses—how does this tell us how Jesus made a way for us? Remember, it's not only about making a way through life, but a way to relationship with our Heavenly Father.

Write a prayer of thanksgiving for who He is.

We often come to God with our requests, but I want to focus on thanking Him this Advent season. No matter what we are going through, there is always something to be thankful for. I love to focus this prayer of thanksgiving on the characteristics of God in that particular passage.

(Optional) Go Deeper questions

Hebrews is a deep book, and we could spend hours diving into the truths written in these verses. If you have time and want to—go for it! But do not let the enemy shame you if you can't. Listen, God's Word is powerful and has purpose. He promises to fulfill that purpose every time we sit down and open our Bibles. No, we won't always have an emotional, big "aha" moment, but He is planting seeds of truth each time we are obedient to open our Bibles. I've found the more I read and study God's Word this way, it increases my desire to be in His Word; I learn more; and I'm changed from the inside-out. It's worth the work—even in a busy season.

Remember

In the back of the book on page 107, you'll find a section to remember and reflect back on this year. This is one of my favorite practices at the end of the year. It's important to look back over the year, to recognize the places where you saw God move, and to see His character on display. There's also a place to look forward to the coming year. We are commanded again and again in Scripture to remember. I encourage you to find a quiet moment before the New Year to go through those questions. Pray, and ask the Holy Spirit to help you remember (it's His job—John 14:26).

Devotionals

Throughout the book, I included devotionals for some of the passages from Hebrews. Several years ago, my family went through a crisis as my husband was diagnosed with an autoimmune disease (Praise God he is doing well!). Many of these words were written during the hardship of that year, especially that Christmas. I was facing feelings of fear, a loss of control, unmet expectations, and I found myself overwhelmed by all of it.

But Jesus.
He never left me.
He never let me go.
His light was never overcome.
He does the same for you.

Additional Resources

While I did not include devotionals for each chapter in this book, I do have teachings available on Season 6 of the Feasting on Truth podcast. Each podcast dives deeper into the whole chapter, provides cultural commentary, and helps explain the meaning behind the passages. You can find more information at FeastingOnTruth.com/WayMaker.

I also highly recommend *Is Jesus Worth It?* by Stacey Thacker. Stacey is a gifted author and teacher and the ease with which she writes of difficult, deep things is refreshing and helps bring clarity.

I am so excited for you this Advent season. I want you to know that I am praying for you. I am praying that the Holy Spirit will meet you as you read and you will not start the new year the same. I pray that this season is a time of slow, intentional, reverent time with Jesus.

Because of Christ,

Erin H. Warren

simple Christmas

I collapsed onto the couch and stared at my bare Christmas tree. I told myself I would decorate it tomorrow, but in my heart I knew that was a lie. Truthfully, my mind kept going to January when I would have to carefully take every one of those glass ornaments back off the tree. I just couldn't do it. I decided not to decorate the tree that year. In fact, we decided not to decorate at all. I let the kids have their trees in their rooms, but sans ornaments. We had to cancel family photos twice because of illness, and I let go of that perfect Christmas card picture I had in my head. In fact, I let go of Christmas cards all together.

This was my Christmas in 2016—the year my husband, Kris, was diagnosed with an autoimmune disease, and we were in the worst of it. I was carrying a lot for my family, and it felt like the weight of everything fell on me. Christmas is my favorite time of year, but this wasn't going to be the Christmas I had dreamed of.

I struggled seeing photos of happy friends all put together for holiday celebrations on social media. Something inside me ached seeing the professional family photos with the sweet smiles and coordinated outfits. It was hard to see pictures from parties and local festivities and to have to continually say "no" to the invitations. That was the Christmas I wanted, but instead I felt like I was trapped in my own life, looking out the window at the world, wishing my Christmas could be different.

One day, as I shared my frustrations with my friend, Amy, she looked at me and said, "I'm just so excited for your family this Christmas. You've been forced to slow down and become laser-focused, and I can't wait to see come January what God did in your hearts and in your family this season."

And slow down we did. Just for good measure, to make sure we REALLY weren't tempted to add anything to our schedule, Kris broke a toe. Yep. For real. (And then I won't even go into the Great Stomach Bug of 2016 that ripped its way through our family on Christmas Day.)

But Amy was right. What we were able to focus on was the simple truth of Christmas: Jesus, our Savior, humbling himself, taking all of His holiness and shoving it into human skin, becoming like us, walking this earth, dying on the cross, taking on the full wrath of God, taking our punishment, raising to life on the third day, and defeating death. All so we could have relationship with God. He didn't just give us forgiveness and Heaven; He gave us Himself. He didn't sit in Heaven and say, "Get yourself together and perfect, then we will talk about this saving business." Jesus became our Way Maker:

but God shows his love for us in that while we were still sinners,
Christ died for us.
Romans 5:8

And the Word became flesh and dwelt among us, and we have seen his glory,
glory as of the only Son from the Father, full of grace and truth.
John 1:14

That year we weren't caught in the hustle of Christmas. Instead, we slowed down; we did an Advent study as a family; we watched ALL the Christmas movies and read ALL the Christmas books; we had dance parties in our family room. And that bare Christmas tree? As my three young kids brought home Christmas crafts and homemade ornaments, instead of wondering where I'd put them all, they found a home on our tree. By the end of the season, the tree wasn't bare at all. It was covered with sweet reminders from my children that Jesus really was the reason for the season.

Your Christmas may not be the one you hoped for. For some of us, we may be trying to make up for lost time, to fill what was lost with activity and yeses. Can I invite you to a simple Christmas? Despite all that has changed, the simple truth of Christmas remains: Jesus came here. He came to be the Way Maker. I pray this study becomes a guide for you to be able to remember that. I echo Amy's encouragement: allow the simple Christmas to drive your heart to be laser-focused on Jesus, the One who came to give us hope, grace, and mercy.

knowing God

For too many years, I struggled with knowing how to interpret Scripture and apply these ancient words to my life. I did not know that God promises to equip us in studying Scripture through the Holy Spirit. And truthfully, I treated my Bible more like one of those balls you shake, ask a question, flip it over, and find your answer. Too many times I came to Scripture looking for an answer to my question, or I treated it like a yearbook—looking for all the pictures of me.

Then, I began asking a different question, and my entire Bible study and life changed. I asked, *What does this say about God?* This shifted my perspective from a self-centered approach to Scripture (where I am always asking, "What does this mean *to* me or *for* me?") to a God-centered approach—intentionally looking for and seeking out what each passage teaches me about God.

The Bible is not about me; it is first and foremost a book about God, and His name and character are written across every page. Our purpose on earth is to know God and make Him known, to love God and love others. But we can't love what we don't know; we can't worship what we don't know. And the primary way we know God is through His Word. The pursuit of knowledge about God is not optional; it's essential.

On the following pages, you will find two lists to help you: Names of God and Characteristics of God. It's not comprehensive and there are spaces for you to add others as you discover more with each passage you read. Here are ways you can have a God-centered approach to your study:

- Ask, "What characteristics of God do I see in this passage?"

- Ask, "What names of God do I see in this passage?" (His names speak to His character.)

- Complete this sentence: Because God is _____, I can _____.

I understand there are different roles of the Trinity (God the Father, God the Son, God the Holy Spirit), but for the sake of simplicity (and especially as you are beginning), I think of them as One. If you want further help, you can visit www.FeastingOnTruth.com for more information and resources.

names of God

Abba Father

Adonai (Lord, Master)

Alpha and Omega

Bread of Life

Chief Cornerstone

Creator

Deliverer

El Elyon (The Most High God)

El Olam (The Everlasting God)

El Roi (The God Who Sees Me)

El Shaddai (The Lord God Almighty)

Elohim

Emmanuel

Everlasting Father

Great High Priest

Holy One

I AM

King of Kings

Lamb of God

Light of the World

Lion of Judah

Lord of Lords

Mighty God

Morning Star

Prince of Peace

Refuge and Strength

Resurrection and the Life

Savior

Wonderful Counselor

Yahweh Amen (The Lord is Truth)

Yahweh Jireh (The Lord Provides)

Yahweh Nissi (The Lord is my Banner)

Yahweh Raah (The Lord is my Shepherd)

Yahweh Rapha (The Lord Heals)

Yahweh Shalom (The Lord is Peace)

characteristics of God

Abounding in Steadfast Love

Compassionate

Creator

Faithful

Forgiving

Full of Grace

Good

Glorious

Gracious

Guide

Holy

Immutable (Never Changes)

Infinite

Jealous

Just

Kind

Long Suffering/Patient

Love

Merciful

Mighty

Omnipotent (All Powerful)

Omnipresent

Omniscient (All Knowing)

One

Perfect

Protector

Provider

Refuge/Help

Righteous

Self-Sufficient

Slow to Anger

Sovereign

Trustworthy

Truth

Wise

With Us

KNOWING GOD NOTES

Hebrews

CHAPTER 1

KEY VERSES: HEBREWS 1:1-4

Write it out:

Way Maker

What does this tell us about Jesus?

How is He the Way Maker?

Way Maker

HEBREWS 1 NOTES

Write a prayer of thanksgiving for who He is:

Go Deeper:

Even when if feels like everything is falling apart, what comfort does it bring to know Jesus holds all things together?

Way Maker

HEBREWS 1 NOTES

Hebrews

CHAPTER 2

Way Maker

KEY VERSES: HEBREWS 2:1,14-18

Write it out:

Way Maker

HEBREWS 2 NOTES

What does this tell us about Jesus?

How is He the Way Maker?

Way Maker

HEBREWS 2 NOTES

Write a prayer of thanksgiving for who He is:

Way Maker

Go Deeper:

Look up *propitiation* in the dictionary and write the definition. How does Jesus do this for us?

....

....

....

....

....

....

....

Write out Hebrews 2:1. How can you remember Who Jesus is? What does remembering protect you from?

....

....

....

....

....

....

....

....

....

....

....

....

....

Way Maker

HEBREWS 2 NOTES

Hebrews

CHAPTER 3

KEY VERSES: HEBREWS 3:1-6

Write it out:

Way Maker

What does this tell us about Jesus?

_____

_____

_____

_____

_____

_____

_____

_____

_____

How is He the Way Maker?

_____

_____

_____

_____

_____

_____

_____

_____

_____

_____

_____

_____

_____

_____

_____

Write a prayer of thanksgiving for who He is:

Go Deeper:

How is Jesus the better and more perfect Moses? ....

....

....

....

....

....

....

....

....

Read vv. 7-14. How do we help each other in continuing to follow Jesus? ....

....

....

....

....

....

....

....

....

....

....

....

....

....

....

Way Maker

HEBREWS 3 NOTES

today

When Kris and I were first married, we were your typical newlyweds: on top of the world and madly in love. When some would see us, they would remark how cute we were. "But just wait," they would say. Once real life settled in … when we had kids … when we had years behind us … that would change. They said the spark would fade.

Well, I, being the uber positive, steadfast girl I am, was really annoyed with that. I would show them. Kris and I began to tell ourselves every morning:

You know what? Someday we may have problems, but it's not going to be today.

My prayer was that I'd wake up in 40 years and still be saying that. Someday maybe, but not today. Marriage requires a daily commitment.

Our faith requires us to approach each day with a similar mindset. This is what the author of Hebrews is talking about in chapter three. He reminds them to look to Jesus:

Therefore, holy brothers, you who share in a heavenly calling, consider Jesus,
the apostle and high priest of our confession, who was faithful to him who
appointed him, just as Moses also was faithful in all God's house.
Hebrews 3:1-2

The Greek word used for *consider* means "to consider attentively, fix one's eyes or mind upon"[1]. In chapter two, he said something similar; he said to pay close attention to Jesus lest we drift away. He's reiterating again to keep looking to Jesus, keep turning your mind to Him, and keep your eyes fixed on Jesus. If we don't, we will naturally move away.

We don't move closer to God on accident. We move closer to God by training our mind to actively stay on Him.

---

1   https://biblehub.com/greek/2657.htm

Then the author reminds them of a familiar story and a familiar passage:

> *But exhort one another every day, as long as it is called "today," that none of you may be hardened by the deceitfulness of sin. For we have come to share in Christ, if indeed we hold our original confidence firm to the end. As it is said, "Today, if you hear his voice, do not harden your hearts as in the rebellion." For who were those who heard and yet rebelled? Was it not all those who left Egypt led by Moses? And with whom was he provoked for forty years? Was it not with those who sinned, whose bodies fell in the wilderness? And to whom did he swear that they would not enter his rest, but to those who were disobedient? So we see that they were unable to enter because of unbelief.*
> Hebrews 3:13-19

The Israelites left Egypt bound for Canaan (the Promised Land) on a 40-year journey that should have taken 11 days. *Eleven days!* They witnessed the power of God through ten plagues. They saw God's glory in the form of a pillar of cloud by day and a pillar of fire by night. They walked across the Red Sea on *dry* land. They watched walls of water collapse on the army of Pharaoh.

How is it that these people, who saw so many amazing acts of God, could stray so far in their faith that God allowed them to wander the wilderness for 40 years and never enter the Promised Land?

They hardened their hearts. Not quickly. Not in an instant. But, over time, they drifted away.

They most likely didn't make a daily choice to honor their commitment. They didn't turn their minds to God. *Every. Day.*

Did you catch what the author said in verse 13? *Today.* Today if you hear His voice, don't harden your hearts. *Today* encourage one another. (He quotes excerpts from Psalm 95 three times.)

What if part of our daily commitment to God is also a daily commitment to each other?

What if we aren't supposed to wait until someone needs encouragement?

What if part of the safeguard against a hardening heart is *daily* encouraging one another to make the commitment every day to say, "Someday I may drift, but it's not going to be today."

Has my faith waivered? You bet. Have I questioned God and wondered why I'm walking the path I am? More than I care to admit. Have I faced hardships? Yes.

Am I in danger of a hardened heart? Unfortunately, yes. We all are. But because of a commitment to my Father, the bumps and twists in the road draw me closer.

Don't miss the Promised Land. Don't miss what God has waiting for you because you drifted and ended up hardening your heart.

Start *Today.* Consider Jesus. Turn your mind to Jesus. Fix your mind, your eyes on Jesus. I pray you wake up years from now still saying:

Someday maybe, but not today.

Hebrews

CHAPTER 4

KEY VERSES: HEBREWS 4:14-16

Write it out:

What does this tell us about Jesus?

How is He the Way Maker?

Way Maker

HEBREWS 4 NOTES

Write a prayer of thanksgiving for who He is:

Go Deeper:

How does knowing Jesus suffered everything we suffer bring comfort to you?

Way Maker

HEBREWS 4 NOTES

our great high priest

Tears began falling down my cheeks as my son's teacher shared what happened in class that morning. Each day, the class starts with prayer requests and praise reports. The kids stick their requests up on the board, and she explained how the children excitedly get to move their requests from the prayer side to the praise side when their prayer is answered.

My sweet boy had asked for prayer for his daddy, but as his teacher relayed the words that came next, I couldn't hold those tears back.

"My daddy is sick, but I don't know when we will be able to move him to the praise board. He's going to be sick for a long time."

Maybe you find yourself in a similar situation: a long-term prayer request, a situation that seems endless, a hurt that won't go away, and you are wondering when your prayer requests can move to the praise board. But even on the days that seem rocky, when our dreams are shattered, and we are desperately trying to hold on for dear life, Jesus never leaves our side. Our Great High Priest has been good to us, and this verse has been one of my greatest comforts:

> *Since then we have a great high priest who has passed through the heavens, Jesus, the Son of God, let us hold fast our confession. For we do not have a high priest who is unable to sympathize with our weaknesses, but one who in every respect has been tempted as we are, yet without sin. Let us then with confidence draw near to the throne of grace, that we may receive mercy and find grace to help in time of need.*
> Hebrews 4:14-16

Mercy. Grace.

In times of need, God doesn't just leave us hanging. He doesn't let us suffer just for suffering's sake. He understands our suffering because He too suffered. We can confidently come to Him, and He freely gives us mercy and grace.

In verse 16 above—"find grace to help us in our time of need"—the Greek word used for *help* is actually a nautical term and the only other place you see it in the New Testament is in Acts

27:17. Paul was in the storm on his way to Rome and it says, "they used supports to undergird the ship." The word *support* is the same word as *help* used in Hebrews[1]. During storms, sailors would take rope or chains and wrap them around the boat to literally hold it together as the waves beat against it. That's what *undergird* means: "to strengthen; secure, as by passing a rope or chain under and around[2]."

That is the help the author of Hebrews is talking about—it means that God wraps grace around us to hold us together during the storms of life. It means that when the wind and waves are beating on our lives from all sides, and we fear we aren't going to make it through, His grace holds us together; His grace supports us; His grace strengthens us; His grace keeps us secure. It doesn't stop the waves from coming, but it keeps us from falling apart. I didn't need to hold the pieces together; Jesus was already doing that. And He's doing that for you as well.

1   https://www.blueletterbible.org/lexicon/g996/kjv/tr/0-1/
2   https://www.blueletterbible.org/lexicon/g5269/kjv/tr/0-1/

Hebrews

CHAPTER 5

Way Maker

KEY VERSES: HEBREWS 5:7-10

Write it out:

Way Maker

HEBREWS 5 NOTES

What does this tell us about Jesus?

How is He the Way Maker?

Way Maker

Write a prayer of thanksgiving for who He is:

HEBREWS 5 NOTES

Go Deeper:

Read vv. 1-5. How is Jesus our High Priest?

_____

_____

_____

_____

_____

_____

_____

_____

Read Genesis 14:17-24. Who was Melchizedek?

_____

_____

_____

_____

_____

_____

_____

_____

_____

_____

Way Maker

HEBREWS 5 NOTES

Hebrews

CHAPTER 6

KEY VERSES: HEBREWS 6:17-20

Write it out:

Way Maker

HEBREWS 6 NOTES

What does this tell us about Jesus?

_____
_____
_____
_____
_____
_____
_____
_____
_____

How is He the Way Maker?

_____
_____
_____
_____
_____
_____
_____
_____
_____
_____
_____
_____
_____
_____

Way Maker

Write a prayer of thanksgiving for who He is:

Go Deeper:

What characteristics of God the Father do we see in this passage?...

....

....

....

....

....

....

....

....

....

....

....

....

....

....

....

....

....

....

....

....

....

....

....

Way Maker

HEBREWS 6 NOTES

hope

My oldest son woke up with a fever; he wouldn't be going to school. I got in the car to take my daughter to school. I turned the key in the ignition. Nothing. We quickly switched to Kris' car and off we went. Later that morning, we tried jumping my car. The battery wouldn't charge. Kris, who during this time was at the height of his battle against an autoimmune disease, drove to the auto store—it was a bad battery and thankfully under warranty. He drove back home, but when he went to put the battery in, he realized the guy at the store gave him the wrong battery. By now, there wasn't enough time for him to go back to exchange the battery. I got home from picking up my daughter, and Kris immediately left to go exchange the battery. He ran into some pretty heavy construction traffic. It was too much, so he turned around and came home. We desperately needed to go to the grocery store, so dinner was an interesting mix. Finally, we gave up on getting to the auto store that night. Kris went to pull his car into the garage to discover he now had a flat tire. We called the shop. They didn't have an opening for three days, but maybe, just maybe, if he got there right at 7am the next morning, they could squeeze him in. My two-year-old poured his milk on the couch. My seven-year-old was on the verge of tears because he just didn't feel well. Kris and I were done.

You've probably had days like these—where nothing seems to go right and you're exhausted, beat down, D-O-N-E; all you want to do is crawl into bed and get the day over with.

We decided to put the kids to bed early because we had nothing left. I went into my four-year-old daughter's room. She bounded across her room, grabbed her purple Bible, and plopped down on the floor. "I need to read to my little friends, Mommy." I was so tempted in my exhaustion to say no, that she needed to brush her teeth and get to bed. But instead, I let her. She opened her Bible, flipping the pages. "I have to find the right one" (flip, flip flip); "here it is!" Then she said, "I don't know the story, but I can sing the words!" And she started to speak/sing, "Away in a manager, no crib for a bed, the little Lord Jesus lay down His sweet head. The stars in the sky look down where He lay. The little Lord Jesus asleep on the hay." (I did chuckle at the thought of "Away in a Manger" being in the Bible.)

With a sigh, I looked down at her Bible and saw the title page for 1 Kings, and I felt Him whisper: "I am the ONE KING. And I'm still on the throne."

Our King Jesus came here. Not as a great ruler, not into a wealthy family or a palace or even a nice suburban home. He didn't even have a crib. He lost his father. He lost a friend. He was falsely accused. He suffered. He was hungry. He was tempted. He wept. He was abandoned. He was beaten. He came to die. He came for you. He came to give us hope. And not just any hope:

We have this as a sure and steadfast anchor of the soul, a hope that enters into
the inner place behind the curtain, where Jesus has gone as a forerunner on
our behalf, having become a high priest forever after the order of Melchizedek.
Hebrews 6:19-20

Melchizedek was a king, but also a high priest in Salem (for more, see Genesis 14). Here, the author of Hebrews points us to this story because Jesus is the more perfect Melchizedek: both King and High Priest. And Jesus, being our Great High Priest, went behind the curtain—the place where only the earthly high priest could go once a year to make a sacrifice and ask forgiveness for the sins of all people, the place where God's glory dwelled—and became the intermediary for us. And because Jesus did that for us, we have hope. Not just fluffy, wishful thinking, fairy dust, wavering, "gee, it sure would be nice if that happened" hope.

Sure. Steadfast. Anchoring. Hope.

This hope is what holds us firmly in place. Like an anchor secures a ship, keeping it from drifting away, so is the truth that Jesus went on our behalf and did what no other high priest had done before: secured our position eternally with our Father. I should also mention that Salem is Hebrew for "peace", and most scholars believe this city is in the same location as Jerusalem. So not only is Jesus an anchor of hope for eternity, but He came, ultimately sacrificing Himself in the city of peace, so that we may have peace for eternity too.

I have said these things to you, that in me you may have peace. In the world
you will have tribulation. But take heart; I have overcome the world.
John 16:33

Oh sweet friends, I don't know where you are today. I don't know what trouble you are facing. But I do know this: Jesus is with you. Take heart. He is anchoring you with hope and covering you with peace. He is our ONE King, Great High Priest, and He is holding you in place. And He has overcome.

Hebrews

CHAPTER 7

Way Maker

KEY VERSES: HEBREWS 7:22-28

Write it out:

Way Maker

HEBREWS 7 NOTES

What does this tell us about Jesus?

How is He the Way Maker?

Write a prayer of thanksgiving for who He is:

Go Deeper:

How is the sacrifice Jesus offered better and more perfect than the one the priests used to offer?

Way Maker

HEBREWS 7 NOTES

Hebrews

CHAPTER 8

Way Maker

HEBREWS 8 NOTES

KEY VERSES: HEBREWS 8:1-7

Write it out:

Way Maker

What does this tell us about Jesus?

How is He the Way Maker?

Way Maker

HEBREWS 8 NOTES

Write a prayer of thanksgiving for who He is:

Go Deeper:

What is the definition of the word *shadow*?

How are the old sacrificial system and the temple a shadow pointing us to Jesus?

Way Maker

HEBREWS 8 NOTES

Hebrews

CHAPTER 9

KEY VERSES: HEBREWS 9:11-14; 24-28

Write it out:

Way Maker

HEBREWS 9 NOTES

What does this tell us about Jesus?

How is He the Way Maker?

Way Maker

HEBREWS 9 NOTES

Write a prayer of thanksgiving for who He is:

Go Deeper:

What hope do we have for eternity because of Jesus making the way?

Way Maker

HEBREWS 9 NOTES

Hebrews

CHAPTER 10

KEY VERSES: HEBREWS 10:19-25

Write it out:

Way Maker

HEBREWS 10 NOTES

What does this tell us about Jesus?

How is He the Way Maker?

Way Maker

HEBREWS 10 NOTES

Write a prayer of thanksgiving for who He is:

Way Maker

Go Deeper:

How should we respond because of what Jesus did for us?

Way Maker

HEBREWS 10 NOTES

who does that?!

Some women come into your life, and you are never the same for it. Lynda was one of those women. It was an unlikely friendship. Her kids and I grew up in school together, and she always loved to tell people how she had known me since I was knee-high (which is now funny because I am about 8 inches taller than Lynda!). We worked together at the same church, and I led a Bible study during our lunch break. It started large, but eventually it dwindled down to just Lynda and me. We would meet one morning a week before work to study God's Word together. Today, she is one of the reasons I love His Word so much.

Every step of the way, Lynda was there. When God called me to start Feasting on Truth, Lynda was still right there—praying, showing up, even leading groups when I asked. (Which, I might add, she always did reluctantly. Lynda thought she was better at leading children than she was at leading women. This was not true at all.) She had a way with words, and she used them generously to encourage others—no matter what age they happened to be.

The years 2020 and 2021 brought losses for many of us: jobs, dreams, plans, people. Lynda was one of my great losses. She passed away on September 12, 2021. I know the moment she breathed her last here and experienced the wholeness of Heaven, she was probably tracking down John to thank him for penning her life verse (John 16:33) and looking for Peter and Paul, asking them ALL the questions.

Lynda had such an incredible perspective of our Way Maker. In Bible study, she would often exclaim, "Who does that?!" as we witnessed the incredible kindness of our God. Our studies were full of those moments: when Jesus would go out of His way to meet a woman at a well or step out in a garden to face those who came to arrest Him saying, "Here I AM." She would inevitably say, "Who does that?!" Only Jesus. And she knew Him well.

Hebrews 10 is one big "Who does that?!" passage.

We have a God who gave us a picture of what He was going to do (a shadow) and was faithful to follow through. The author of Hebrews calls the law a *shadow* of the true form. A shadow is not something to grab or hold. A shadow is just a darkened outline of an object. It's not the real thing; it's a representation of the real thing. He is comparing what the priests had to do to ask forgiveness for sins (the shadow) to how Christ died once for all (the true form).

One time each year, the high priest (and only the high priest) would enter the presence of God and offer a sacrifice to ask forgiveness for the sins of Israel for that year (see Leviticus 16). The presence of God dwelled in the Tabernacle and later in Solomon's temple in what was called the Holy of Holies or the Most Holy Place. It was at the heart of the Tabernacle and temple and sectioned off by a huge curtain (or veil). While the Bible doesn't say exactly how large or thick the curtain was, tradition suggests it was about 15-18 feet high and was as thick as your hand. Only the high priest could go behind this curtain into the presence of God, only one time a year, and only after a strict cleansing process. But all of that was a shadow. The real Savior was coming!

My favorite part of the redemption story comes just as Jesus breathes His last on the cross:

> *Now from the sixth hour there was darkness over all the land until the ninth*
> *hour. And about the ninth hour Jesus cried out with a loud voice, saying, "Eli,*
> *Eli, lema sabachthani?" that is, "My God, my God, why have you forsaken*
> *me?" And Jesus cried out again with a loud voice and yielded up his spirit.*
> *And behold, the curtain of the temple was torn in two, from top to bottom.*
> *And the earth shook, and the rocks were split.*
> Matthew 27:45-46; 50-51

The moment Jesus died, the tall curtain that couldn't be torn in two tore from top to bottom. No one cut it; it was not ripped by human hands. God, through Jesus, made a way for us to have intimate access to Him like never before.

Who does that?!

> *Therefore, brothers, since we have confidence to enter the holy places by the*
> *blood of Jesus, by the new and living way that he opened for us through the*
> *curtain, that is, through his flesh, and since we have a great priest over the*
> *house of God, let us draw near with a true heart in full assurance of faith,*
> *with our hearts sprinkled clean from an evil conscience and our bodies washed*
> *with pure water.*
> Hebrews 10:19-22

We no longer have to stand at a distance! His body, pierced and torn, opened a way for us to draw near. His blood gives us confidence to enter "the holy places." We no longer have to get cleaned up before we can come to God. He meets us where we are. His sacrifice does once and for all what years of sacrifice could never do: bring forgiveness of sins (Hebrews 10:17-18), a finished work (Hebrews 10:12-14), and cleanse us by the blood of His perfect sacrifice (Hebrews 10:22-23).

I will never get over what He did for me. I don't get it. I do not deserve His grace, forgiveness and love. I continually find myself returning to the same pit of sin; and every time, He meets me there, pulls me out and says, "I forgive you. I love you. No matter what."

Who does that?!

Don't settle for the shadow of Christianity. Not one of us is good enough to do it on our own. There is no life He cannot redeem. No one is too far gone. That curtain tore in two so we can draw near to our Creator with confidence. I pray this Christmas you draw close and find time to reflect on what His coming means for us as believers. Hold fast to that confession of hope without wavering. And because He did that, don't miss His call to community either:

> *Let us hold fast the confession of our hope without wavering, for he who promised is faithful. And let us consider how to stir up one another to love and good works, not neglecting to meet together, as is the habit of some, but encouraging one another, and all the more as you see the Day drawing near.*
> Hebrews 10:23-25

I will always be grateful that Lynda never stopped stirring others up toward love and good works. The line of people with a testimony of how she showed up for them, encouraged them, and met with them, is long. She kept pointing people to our "Who Does That?!" God. Even when our study dwindled to two, she didn't neglect to show up. Even when she was walking through some really hard things, she kept being obedient to God's call. That's the kind of woman I want to be. It's my prayer for you too. Let's keep showing up because when we needed it most, our Way Maker showed up for us.

Who does that?!

Hebrews

CHAPTER 11

HEBREWS 11 NOTES

KEY VERSES: HEBREWS 11:1-3, 6

Write it out:

Way Maker

HEBREWS 11 NOTES

What does this tell us about Jesus?

How is He the Way Maker?

Way Maker

HEBREWS 11 NOTES

Write a prayer of thanksgiving for who He is:

Way Maker

Go Deeper:

What is the definition of *faith*?

....

....

....

....

....

Pick 2-3 of the names mentioned in this "Hall of Faith" and look up their stories. What hope do you have because of their testimony?

....

....

....

....

....

....

....

....

....

....

....

....

....

....

Way Maker

HEBREWS 11 NOTES

Hebrews

CHAPTER 12

KEY VERSES: HEBREWS 12:1-2, 22-29

Write it out:

Way Maker

HEBREWS 12 NOTES

What does this tell us about Jesus?

How is He the Way Maker?

Way Maker

HEBREWS 12 NOTES

Write a prayer of thanksgiving for who He is:

Go Deeper:

Read Mark 13:24-27. What hope do you have in knowing His Kingdom cannot be shaken?

Way Maker

HEBREWS 12 NOTES

the shaking

I felt like I was herding cats. The hands of my kids (ages 2, 4, and 7) were moving faster than I could manage. My husband was at home in bed resting, and there I was at my parents' house trying to make Christmas cookies with my children. I wanted to teach them how you carefully place each cookie cutter near the edge to get the most out of the dough. Instead, cookie cutters were haphazardly smooshed wherever their hearts desired. I was frantically jumping in as cut pieces of dough were carelessly picked up and thrown onto the cookie sheet. Stars were misshaped. Hearts were squished. Gingerbread men were losing their heads. I was about to lose my mind.

That's how I felt about my life right then: I was frantically trying to manage it all, but I couldn't. Balls kept dropping. Everything seemed out of my control. I could not hold it all together—not even the poor gingerbread men.

That was a year of shaking for me. I felt God shaking me as the waves of hardship, trials, setbacks, and unknowns continued to pound. With each wave, things began spilling out of me, and they weren't always pretty. It began to reveal the ugliness of sin in my heart. Until these days, I had fancied myself a "good girl." But as my trials continued on, God continued to shake out of me what could be shaken—all for the purpose of showing me what cannot be shaken.

At that time his voice shook the earth, but now he has promised, "Yet once more I will shake not only the earth but also the heavens." This phrase, "Yet once more," indicates the removal of things that are shaken—that is, things that have been made—in order that the things that cannot be shaken may remain.
Hebrews 12:26-27

John Newton, who wrote the hymn "Amazing Grace", often wrote letters to parishioners to encourage them in their faith and encourage them through their hardships. In his book *Newton on the Christian Life*, Tony Reinke points to Newton's idea that trials smoke out our idols.

In other words, trials are designed to prevent us from living at peace with our idols and remaining in sin. Much of our sin appears hidden and dormant until the whip-snap of affliction rouses the indwelling sin to stand up and show itself, or stand up and hiss, or stand up and strike. It is more necessary for us to see the sins remaining in our hearts and to flee to Christ for grace than it is to live blissfully ignorant of the cancers in our soul. And we know this, Newton explains, because God sends afflictions into our lives. Trials are medicines of kindness applied to serious diseases called indwelling sins.[1]

Idol work has been a hard yet necessary practice in my relationship with God. An idol is anything we place value on above God and anything we turn to instead of God. It can be something physical, an action, or even an emotion.

That Christmas began to reveal to me how much value I had placed on the events and traditions of Christmas over the Author of Christmas. It reminded me that He is sovereign over it all. It reminded me that He does not ask me to hold everything together; He is already doing that. It reminded me that I do not need to know the future; all I need to remember is that He goes before me and behind me. He hems me in.

Instead, He asks me to throw off all that hinders me; to let go of the weights that hold me down and run with endurance after Him (Hebrews 12:1-2). Sometimes throwing off what hinders me comes at the hands of trials. It comes in times of suffering. It comes with shaking.

I have a love-hate relationship with the word *endurance*, but we see the call to it (or your version may say *perseverance*) over and over in Scripture. The Greek word for *endurance* means "steadfast, patiently waiting"[2]. It comes from two root words meaning "under" and "remain".

I don't want to stay under. I want to bypass the hurt. I want to skirt around the pain. I want to get out from under the hardships. But that's not what we are called to do. Like the old children's story tells us, we can't go over it. We can't go under it. We can't go around it. We have to go through it. The only way through is through. But God continues to use these hardships to grow me, to build endurance, to refine my character; and the result is hope (Romans 5:3-5). That's what Christmas is all about: Hope. Not a wish or a flimsy desire or something arbitrary. It's that Hebrews 6, sure and steadfast hope—hope that does not disappoint or put us to shame. Hope that

1   Reinke, T. (2015). Newton on the Christian Life: To Live Is Christ. United States: Crossway. p. 182
2   https://biblehub.com/greek/5281.htm

one day, we will be in eternity with Christ. There will be no more tears or death or mourning or weeping or pain. Hope that all things will be made new. God will dwell with us and us with Him.

What remains true and what cannot be shaken are the things of God. What a glorious promise! And, as the author of Hebrews says, our response is worship. We are grateful. We are in awe of our God, who made a way through Jesus for us to receive that which is unchanging and unmovable and unshakable (Hebrews 12:28-29). And let's face it: we were going to bite the head of the gingerbread man off anyway.

Hebrews

CHAPTER 13

Way Maker

HEBREWS 13 NOTES

KEY VERSES: HEBREWS 13:20-21

Write it out:

Way Maker

HEBREWS 13 NOTES

What does this tell us about Jesus?

How is He the Way Maker?

Way Maker

HEBREWS 13 NOTES

Write a prayer of thanksgiving for who He is:

Way Maker

HEBREWS 13 NOTES

Go Deeper:

Read the entire chapter. Because of who He is and how He has made a way, how should our life look different?

Way Maker

HEBREWS 13 NOTES

remember

Over and over in Scripture, we see God call His people to remember. They built a stone altar to remember crossing the Jordan. The Israelites carry a jar of manna to remember God's provision in the wilderness. They celebrate Passover to remember God saving them from Egypt. We celebrate the Lord's Supper to remember Christ's death on the cross. We celebrate Christmas to remember His coming. We celebrate Easter to remember His resurrection. Recording and remembering is an important practice in our faith. It's how we can look back and see where God worked in our lives and how we've changed as a result.

Hebrews 2:1 says, *"We must pay much closer attention to what we have heard lest we drift away."* The Greek word for *pay much closer* literally means to "turn our minds to". We must continually and physically turn our minds from our problems, circumstances, and sin, and instead turn to Him: Who He is, His character, what He has done for us, and what we have learned about Him. That's what keeps us from drifting away. That is what keeps us following Him even when life is hard.

One of my favorite times to remember is at the end of the calendar year. I love to look back on the year. As the saying goes, hindsight is 20/20, and it's often at the end of the year I can look back and see how far God took me during those last 12 months. These next pages are a guide—a way for you to reflect on the past year and see the hand of God.

It can be hard to do this, but thankfully God doesn't call us to remember without providing the help we need to do so. In John 14:26, Jesus promises, *"But the Helper, the Holy Spirit, whom the Father will send in my name, he will teach you all things and bring to your remembrance all that I have said to you."* The Holy Spirit is there to guide you and help you remember.

You do not have to work through the following pages all at once. I recommend getting away, if even for an hour, to a quiet place with no distractions. Our tendency in these types of exercises is to focus on the physical things God did or what He physically or materially gave us. But I challenge you to use the list of God's names and characteristics on pages 12-13. Where did you see Him display His character in your life? Where did you see His grace, goodness, gentleness, patience, etc?

The older I get the more I realize life is not a series of peaks and valleys but rather a dance between joy and sorrow. They can, and often do, co-exist. Good and hard are not mutually exclusive. Even in the midst of hard years, I know God never ceased being God. As my friend, Amy, says, "Find Jesus in the junk." Pray. Invite the Holy Spirit to help you remember and bring to mind who God is and what He did for you.

REMEMBER LIFE

What was hard this year?

REMEMBER

What was good this year?

Way Maker

REMEMBER

What memories do I want to remember?

REMEMBER HABITS

What did I stop doing that I do not want to start again? ....

_____

_____

_____

_____

_____

_____

_____

_____

_____

_____

_____

_____

_____

_____

_____

_____

_____

_____

_____

_____

_____

_____

What did I start doing that I do not want to stop?

REMEMBER GOD

How did God surprise me this year?

How did God provide for me this year?

How did God change my perspective this year?

REMEMBER

How did God show His character in my life this year?

REFLECT BACK/LOOK FORWARD

What was my word/goal for this year? What did God teach me?

What is my word/goal for next year? Why?

feasting at the table

There's something about Christmas that screams cookies. I can remember as a young girl baking cookies with four generations: my great-grandmother, my grandmother, my mom, and us kids. We made the same family recipes year after year: buckeye balls, jam dots, sugar cookies, and gingerbread cookies. It's a tradition we've continued to carry on now for more years than I can count. I love passing on these recipes to my own children.

Food evokes memories. I can take one bite of a buckeye ball and instantly be taken back to Christmas-cookie baking. There's something powerful about being in the kitchen together, working together, and eating together. It creates a sense of belonging. It draws people together. And at the end of the process, there's something (hopefully) delicious to enjoy. (If not, maybe you'll get a good #kitchenfail story out of it.) But all this seems to be exponentially increased during family holidays.

My favorite cookies are chocolate ones, but a few Christmases ago I discovered peppermint chips—and these Dark Chocolate Peppermint Cookies were born. I mean, what could be more Christmas than peppermint and chocolate?! They are delicate and surprisingly light. The refreshing peppermint balances the richness of the dark chocolate, and they are now my husband's favorite cookie. Because they are chocolate, it's hard to tell when they are done. Every oven is different, but mine is precisely 8.5 minutes. If you're unsure, after removing them from the oven let them sit on the tray for a couple minutes before moving to the cooling rack.

This recipe makes a lot of cookies (about 4 dozen), so feel free to share or you can freeze the extra cookies. Enjoy, and happy feasting!

DARK CHOCOLATE PEPPERMINT COOKIES

Time: About 45 minutes
Yield: About 48 small cookies

INGREDIENTS

2 cups unbleached all-purpose flour
1 teaspoon baking soda
1 teaspoon baking powder
½ teaspoon salt
½ cup unsweetened cocoa powder

1 cup unsalted butter, softened
1 ¼ c sugar
2 tablespoons molasses
2 eggs
1 teaspoon vanilla

1 bag peppermint chips
1 bag dark chocolate chips

flake sea salt

INSTRUCTIONS

1. Preheat the oven to 375 degrees. Line two cookie sheets with parchment paper.

2. In a medium bowl, whisk together flour, baking soda, baking powder, salt, and cocoa powder. Set aside.

3. In the bowl of a stand mixer with paddle attachment, cream the butter and sugar at medium-high speed until light and fluffy, about 3 minutes. (If you do not have a stand mixer, you can use a hand mixer instead.)

4. Reduce speed to low. Add molasses, scraping down the sides of the bowl.

5. Add the eggs, one at a time, mixing well. Then add the vanilla.

6. With the mixer still on low, gradually add the flour mixture, scraping down the sides of the bowl periodically.

7. Turn off mixer, remove bowl, and thoroughly stir in the chocolate and peppermint chips.

8. Spoon dough onto cookie sheets about 2-3 inches apart using a tablespoon cookie scoop (about the size of a dinner spoon). Gently press the top of each cookie so it's flat. Sprinkle with flake sea salt. You should be able to fit about 12 cookies per sheet.

9. Bake at 375 degrees for 8-9 minutes. Let cool on tray for about 4 minutes before moving to a cooling rack. Repeat with the remaining dough.

about Erin

Erin H. Warren is passionate about equipping and encouraging women to discover God's truths for themselves. She leads and teaches Bible Studies, speaks, and writes. She and her husband, Kris, have three littles (who aren't so little anymore), and they live in Central Florida. She loves coffee, a house full of people and a table full of food, and hopes tacos never go out of style. Here's where you can keep up with Erin:

Website: www.ErinHWarren.com
Instagram: @erinhwarren & @feastingontruth
YouTube: www.youtube.com/c/erinhwarren

Made in United States
North Haven, CT
10 October 2022